The Perfect Picnic
outdoor entertaining with style

The Perfect Picnic

outdoor entertaining with style

Anita Louise Crane

Sterling Publishing Co., Inc. New York
A Sterling/Chapelle Book

Chapelle Ltd.

Owner: Jo Packham

Editor: Linda Orton

Staff: Areta Bingham, Kass Burchett, Ray Cornia, Marilyn Goff, Holly Hollingsworth, Susan Jorgensen, Barbara Milburn, Karmen Quinney, Cindy Stoeckl, Kim Taylor, Sara Toliver, Desirée Wybrow

Photo Stylists: Anita Crane
                 Jill Dahlberg

Photography: Anita Crane
              Scot Zimmerman, Zimmerman Photography
              Kevin Dilley, Hazen Imaging, Inc.

Library of Congress Cataloging-in-Publication Available

10 9 8 7 6 5 4 3 2 1

A Sterling/Chapelle Book

Published by Sterling Publishing Co., Inc.
387 Park Avenue South, New York, NY 10016
© 2002 by Anita Louise Crane
Distributed in Canada by Sterling Publishing
% Canadian Manda Group, One Atlantic Avenue, Suite 105
Toronto, Ontario, Canada M6K 3E7
Distributed in Great Britain and Europe by Cassell PLC
Wellington House, 125 Strand, London WC2R 0BB, England
Distributed in Australia by Capricorn Link (Australia) Pty. Ltd.
P.O. Box 704, Windsor, NSW 2756, Australia
Printed in China
All Rights Reserved

Sterling ISBN 0-8069-5479-5

If you have any questions or comments, please contact:

Chapelle Ltd., Inc.
P.O. Box 9252
Ogden, UT 84409

Phone: (801) 621-2777
FAX: (801) 621-2788
e-mail: chapelle@chapelleltd.com
website: www.chapelleltd.com

In fondest memories of Amy Townsend, "Gram," and her tree house.

Anita Louise Crane has been designing, creating, photographing, marketing, selling, and writing about collectible teddy bears since 1981. Her teddy bear creations are known worldwide through coverage in collectors' and trade magazines, including *Teddy Bears and Friends, Creative Needle,* England's *Hugletts,* and Australia's *Dolls, Bears and Collectibles.*

She teaches children's book illustration classes at the University of Utah. In addition, Anita has written, and illustrated eight books (Sterling/Chapelle, Ltd., Publishing): *Teddy Bear Magic, Making Adorable Teddy Bears, Two-Hour® Dolls' Clothes, Adorable Furniture for Dolls & Teddy Bears, Two-Hour® Scrap Crafts, Decorating with Seashells,* and *Victorian Chic.*

Anita's artistic productions are as varied as her experiences and interests, with her art and home being featured in several nationally known magazines which include: *Romantic Homes* and *Victoria.* Her watercolor images have appeared on Hallmark Cards (Ambassador), Lovelace, Ltd., greeting cards, and magazine covers.

Currently, she is dedicated—passionately so—to building a career as a children's book illustrator where she is particularly gifted in the drawing and painting of teddy bears along with other animals. She has already been signed for additional books, one being a children's book, *No Go Outside.*

Anita lives with her husband and cat, Raisen. She is the mother of four grown children and the proud grandmother of nine. Spending time in the beautiful mountains and enjoying her art fills up much of her days.

I would like to thank Dixie Barber for once again allowing us into her lovely home and garden to photograph pictures for this book, as well as a thank you to my editors, Kristi Torsak and Linda Orton. Scot Zimmerman has done a wonderful job with his photographs, thank you Scot. A special thanks to my brother, Jim Speck, and also to my husband, Bruce, who always allows me to fill our home with props during the process of writing a book. Thanks to all of you.
–Anita Crane

TABLE OF CONTENTS

introduction 8

chapter 1
in the Basket 10

chapter 2
and the Accessories 24

chapter 3
for a PICNIC 44

chapter 4
in the Woods 52

chapter 5
in the Garden 60

chapter 6
on the Porch 78

chapter 7
in Unusual Places 86

chapter 8
ON THE ROAD 100

chapter 9
in the home 108

chapter 10
for the Children 118

metric tables 130

Acknowledgments............... 131

INDEX 132

introduction

As you open this book, you might ask yourself, "What is the perfect picnic?" Take something to eat outside, or inside somewhere other than the regular dining area, and you have a picnic. Take dashing elegance, and a carefree manner and you have style. Blend the two together and you have a special way to celebrate life.

Everyone loves picnics; and when we get the opportunity to dine with fabulous views, unusual sounds, and enticing smells, we are not only eating for physical nourishment, we are feeding our souls. Finding that perfect place and adding a few special touches awakens the senses; and it is an occasion like this that builds relationships and brings about memorable conversations.

When one strolls through a museum of European Impressionist paintings created by the great artists, elegant outdoor dining is often captured. Entire weekends were dedicated to the tradition of picnicking with entertainment, good food, and choice company. The scenes in these paintings may consist of a quilt set out on verdant grass, a secluded flower garden, or a pair of lovers floating on quiet waters. The food in the painting adds color, texture, and taste to the scene. These paintings of long ago observe that food was not the main focus of the afternoon, but a time of festivity and romance. In such settings, people are communicating in a relaxing environment and the experience is a celebration of life and relationships.

Modern-day picnics can have all these qualities and be held in a myriad of places. Why not picnic on the porch, beside the road, or even in bed? Perhaps your park is the roof of a building, or the tailgate of a pickup truck. Imagine the transformation of the seemingly ordinary or less attractive site, such as introducing a pretty tablecloth spread over a workbench in a construction area. Details such as a single rose in a beverage bottle and a hearty deli sandwich will amuse and delight your guests.

Just as you can be creative with the picnic setting, you can be creative with whom you invite along. Picnics don't have to be just for families. Invite new and old neighbors, people from your church, business associates, or some neighborhood children. Mix up the guest list and see what happens!

You might think of a picnic as being a weekend lunch in the summertime. Step out and try having a picnic for any meal of the day, any day of the week, and any day of the year. An impromptu picnic can be a special occasion when we hurriedly packed for an evening hike up a mountain trail to catch the

sunset. Why not call a coworker and have him or her meet you at the park for a sack lunch picnic?

Another way to bring vitality to your picnic is the food itself. You need not serve ordinary picnic food at your picnic. Opt for chilled sparkling grape juice or ready-made punch instead of soda pop. Serve a favorite casserole or Mexican dish instead of cold-cut sandwiches. Skip the potato salad and wow your guests with gazpacho soup. A beautiful or unusual setting, a variety of personalities, an offbeat time of day or day of year, tantalizing food, and the addition of special touches will make your picnic one to be remembered.

"The Perfect Picnic" is full of imaginative picnic ideas, along with tried-and-true picnic recipes and instructions for customized accessories. Use these ideas as stepping-stones to create your very own perfect picnic.

in the *Basket*

Whether you are escaping to a misty lake, hiking a favorite trail, or simply headed out to the garden with a salt shaker, baskets and creative containers can be quite useful for carrying food and other picnic supplies.

I have a collection of antique baskets dating from the early 1900s to present day—some with handles, some without, and some with lids that can be used for a table. Baskets are inexpensive and readily available. At department stores, you can even find picnic baskets complete with plates, cutlery, champagne glasses, floral or checkered napkins, and a tablecloth. Your picnic basket might be made from fabric or be a metal lunch pail. Many people collect metal lunch boxes that were used for school lunches in

days past. Those of us who used them hardly realized that we were actually having a picnic every day in the school yard or lunch room.

You might roll up your food and accessories in a tablecloth, napkin, an old straw hat or, when all else fails, a simple cardboard box or grocery bag. I once knew a lady who found that her plastic laundry basket made an efficient container for her large family picnics. For beach picnics, a cooler works great because it keeps the sand out of the food.

Whatever your choice may be, take extra care to keep hot foods hot and cold foods cold. Always include beverages in a picnic—they can be carried in a plastic jug, or cooler with ice.

types of
Baskets

What, besides a traditional basket, can be used as a picnic basket? As long as it's capable of holding the picnic food and supplies, and it's not too heavy to carry or has wheels, it is limited only to your imagination. A poolside or beach picnic can be packed in big plastic buckets that can be purchased inexpensively at toy stores. Various other toys, such as trucks, boats, baby doll cribs or carriages, turn on the charm for children's picnics or outside parties.

An antique toy wheelbarrow, charming hat boxes, old tin lunch boxes, wicker baskets of all sizes, and a limitless number of other fun and unique picnic containers can be found with a little patience. Flea markets, antique shops, garage or estate sales, craft shows, thrift shops, dime stores, and department stores are examples of places where you can purchase decorative and functional picnic accessories. You may even discover picnic containers by dusting off old boxes and baskets stored in your attic or basement.

Oftentimes, gifts come in beautiful boxes and baskets. Don't throw these lovely containers away after you remove the present. With a few simple alterations, such as replacing an Easter bunny bow with streamers of taffeta, or giving a charming gift box a new coat of paint, these containers can be reused at your next picnic to hold plates, food items, or (if large enough) even the entire picnic.

Planters of all sizes, shapes, and styles hold picnic meals and accessories beautifully and efficiently. Take a simple picnic idea, such as individually bagged lunches, and refine it a little for a picnic sure to please. As seen in the photograph below, a wooden planter carries five brown-bagged lunches, each labeled with name tags and adorned with twine.

A wooden crate or a plastic milk crate can be woven with colorful ribbons. Use your creativity, and you're certain to come up with a picnic basket that's anything but ordinary.

NOT YOUR REGULAR SACK LUNCH

❧ Place provolone cheese, leftover thinly sliced grilled veggies, shredded lettuce, and avocado on a tomato-flavored tortilla at your picnic site. Season with balsamic vinaigrette dressing and roll up like an eggroll.

❧ Serve a pesto pasta salad, made with penne pasta, fresh tomatoes, basil, and a sweet yellow pepper. Make a dressing for the salad by mixing equal parts of pesto and balsamic vinaigrette.

Is your husband or boyfriend a golf nut? Load up his golf clubs and show him a stroke of genius on the green. Metal or plastic golf ball baskets make wonderful picnic baskets, and add some other golf paraphernalia for a romantic picnic for two and—fore!—what a shot!

This idea can be adapted to whatever sport your significant other loves to play or cheer for, so be creative. If they play tennis, pack a surprise picnic in a tennis racquet bag and have them join you for lunch in the stands. If their fancy is football, pack a barbeque-and-beer picnic in a cooler for a parking lot tailgater they won't soon forget.

While he is on the job, a galvanized lunch pail accompanied with a gourmet picnic snack of fresh fruit, cheese, and flavored mineral water paints quite a romantic picture. To enhance the ambience, bring a bouquet of fresh flowers and have classical

music playing in the background. Such a picnic can be arranged anywhere his job carries him.

A quick trip through the drive-through can become a delightful picnic if in the right setting. Take the hamburgers and french fries out of the original bags, fill in with a few side dishes and accessories from home, and place them in a plastic beach bag or other container. Many delis, restaurants, and grocery stores will prepare picnics just for you with a quick phone call. All you have to do is pick up some food and find a park to sit in to bring a sense of relaxation to a wild and harried workday.

the _perfect_ picnic basket

Prepare a picnic basket that is always prepacked with the basics and ready to go. Whether that means your best china, stemware, and silverware, or inexpensive plastic or disposable dishes, it is up to you. The perfect picnic basket may be two different types of baskets packed for whatever picnic occasion may arise. A basket that is ready to go should contain the following items:

- Plates
- Eating utensils
- Glasses or cups
- Tablecloth
- Napkins
- Corkscrew
- Bottle and can openers
- Garbage bags

In addition to the above, the following are also handy to have in a prepacked basket:

- Salt and pepper shakers
- Sugar

- Serving utensils
- Sharp knife
- Vase for flowers
- Plastic zipper bags for leftovers
- Small cutting board or plastic cutting mat
- Insect repellent
- Paper towels or moist towelettes
- Sunscreen
- Matches

Other pertinent supplies for your perfect picnic include:

- Cooler
- Ice and freezer packs
- Thermos

I call the following "comfort items," and if they are stored in a place close to your picnic basket they will be easily accessible.

- Blanket
- Candles and candleholders
- First aid kit
- Folding chairs
- Folding table
- Ground blanket or sheet
- Umbrella

These are just suggestions, the perfect picnic basket will be defined by you and what you want to make a picnic successful. You may find that you have already established traditions calling for items not previously listed. Customizing your basket to fit your needs is the main objective of this chapter.

It is always a good plan to pack ice cubes in a plastic container or plastic bag even if you have freezer packs in the cooler to keep foods chilled. The ice has multiple uses and can be used in drinks or to soothe an itching or stinging insect bite. Plastic jugs or jars, that will fit in the cooler, can be filled and frozen ahead of time. They will keep food cold and provide a cold drink on a hot summer day.

A battery-operated radio or CD player helps to provide atmosphere, while cards or small travel games may provide entertainment for more casual picnics.

Along with the previous suggestions, take into consideration the ages and number of people invited and pack your picnic basket accordingly.

Picnic safety tips

Some of the foremost safety tips that I can give are concerning the storage of picnic foods. Foods that will be served cold should be well chilled or frozen before packing them. They need to be packed with ice or freezer packs in a cooler where they will stay cold until cooking time. Especially take care in keeping raw meats well chilled that will be transported and cooked at the picnic site. Transport coolers inside of an air-conditioned car rather than the trunk on hot days.

Hot foods must be brought to the highest temperature possible and packed in thermos containers or food warmers. Always wrap hot foods in aluminum or store in containers that will retain the heat. Maintaining a temperature of 140°F is imperative. A portable stove to heat foods that are served hot could be used as an alternative to packing hot foods. Care should always be taken with perishable foods such as poultry, mayonnaise, and eggs. It is not advisable to bring home leftovers that may have set out for more than two hours. Always remember, "when in doubt, throw it out." Soap,

THINGS TO CONSIDER

- Take plenty of ice.
- Remember covers to cover food.
- Don't forget hats and sweaters or jackets.
- Always have a flashlight on hand.
- Leave the picnic site clean.

- Do not picnic on private property without permission.
- Keep a watch out for wild animals.
- Dress in bright colors during hunting season.
- Place a sprig of fresh mint on the blanket to deter bees.

water, and towels or moist towelettes are best for keeping hands clean when working with foods. Keep the following additional tips in mind for meat and food items:

❧ Perishable food items should be eaten or stored on ice within two hours of cooking. This includes takeout items such as fried chicken.

❧ Plan to take only the amount of food that can be eaten, so there is no worry about storing leftovers.

❧ When grilling raw meat, remove from the cooler only the amount that will fit on the grill.

❧ Always discard marinade from meats.

❧ Never place cooked meat on the same platter that the raw meat was set on.

❧ Pack raw meats on the bottom of your cooler. This will keep them cooler and also prevent them from dripping onto other food.

❧ Use a separate cooler for drinks to minimize the opening and closing of a cooler that may contain perishable items.

and the Accessories

Picnic accessories include the basic elements that make a picnic manageable and comfortable—plates, napkins, cutlery, a tablecloth, chairs, and any other items that you deem a necessary part of a successful picnic.

A quilt or blanket makes for a perfectly comfortable sit for a picnic on the ground. You will want to place a sheet of plastic underneath the blanket to keep moisture from soaking into the blanket. You can sit directly on the blanket, or bring stadium seats for some added cushion.

If you would rather not sit on the ground, you can use a table and chairs for your picnic. These can be dainty, wooden table sets; a card table and folding chairs; or even a portable table and bench set, available at sporting goods stores.

Umbrellas, available in many different styles and sizes, give protection from the elements. There is even an umbrella that attaches to the back of your vehicle to shade a tailgate picnic. Umbrellas and seat-ing are just the beginning for picnic accessories. Keep in mind the type of picnic you are planning, since you will find there are some accessories that are basic elements and others that are specific to a singular type of picnic.

To make certain you have not forgotten any important picnic accessories, you can imagine your picnic actually happening, from start to finish. Visualize the different menu items, what will be eaten first and what will be eaten last, the sitting arrangements, and so forth. For example, if corn on the cob will be served, you will want to bring butter, salt and pepper, and corn holders. If you plan to serve a bottle of Sauvignon Blanc, you had best remember the corkscrew and the wine glasses.

You've heard the saying, "Practice makes perfect." Well, the more picnics you have, the better you will get at having them. So don't fret if you forget something—improvise—you will probably remember it next time.

China or not

One decision you will have to make is whether to use nice dishes or disposable dishes for your picnic. For the most part, you will want to pair china or stoneware with silverware, and disposable paper plates with plastic utensils.

A picnic using your best china works best if a table is being used. That way, the surface is relatively smooth and still, and accidental spilling and breaking is less likely. Keep in mind that you must hand-wash the china after the picnic.

Everyday stoneware is another option for a picnic. While these dishes are easier to maintain since they can be washed in a dishwasher, you will still be ahead to serve them on a table instead of on a blanket on the ground. China and stoneware add grace and formality to your picnic, and are typically used in picnic spots close to the house.

Easier to transport, disposable paper or plastic dishes can be used for picnics both near and far. No need to wash, simply toss in a garbage bag when finished. These days, disposable dishes come in a variety of patterns, sizes, and qualities. Nice, heavy-weight paper plates with elaborate patterns will cost more than lightweight paper plates. If you opt for the latter, these can be supported with reusable plastic or straw plate holders. You can have matching plates, napkins, bowls, and cups, or you can be creative and mix-match a potpourri of different colors, patterns, and styles.

With their snapping lids and portability, plastic or rubber containers are conventional yet practical accessories for a picnic. You can find containers that are made to hold and serve condiments such as ketchup, ones made for three-layered cakes, as well as anything in between. Dishwasher-safe and virtually unbreakable, such containers have earned a huge following through the years.

Trays are a fun way to display and serve the picnic food. Taking the cafeteria tray many steps further, try serving your next picnic from a hand-painted wooden tray. Or, if you're hosting a garden tea party with your best china, serving the food from an antique silver tray will raise some eyebrows. For an unexpected twist, serve backyard barbeque food

from a muffin-tin tray. It makes a perfect cup holder and the hamburger, cookies, fresh fruit, and carrots seem right at home in their appointed muffin holes. A Frisbee makes an amusing tray for serving a hot dog and corn chips at a picnic.

Even the way you display the silverware or plastic utensils has a bearing on the overall mood of your picnic. Haphazardly tossing the utensils on a blanket is not nearly as impressive as arranging them in a jar, basket, or flowerpot. Wrapping a fork, knife, and spoon in a pretty napkin and securing with a ribbon looks nice and makes the utensils handy to disperse.

Pass the Condiments

Clay or glass bottles make functional and attractive picnic accessories. Bottles like the ones in this photograph can be purchased in flea markets or gift shops, or you might already have some in your home. Using handmade pottery is a wonderful way to add a personal touch to your picnic.

Simply fill the bottles with condiments such as salt, pepper, oil, vinegar, or whatever is appropriate for your menu. Push a cork securely in the opening, and you're ready to go!

Picnic serving dishes

To give your picnic a style of its own, introduce nontraditional and unique accessories. For example, a fondue set is a surprising element to a picnic. However, since the fondue set has its own heat source and the foods made in it are highly transportable, it is actually a versatile and welcome picnic addition.

Likewise, if homemade ice cream sounds great on a summer day, don't leave it behind when you go for a picnic. If you're going somewhere that has electricity, and you won't be too far from your vehicle, you can bring your ice cream maker. Or, if you are fortunate enough to have one of those old-fashioned ice cream makers that are turned by hand, electricity is not an issue. Simply bring the ice cream maker already prepared with the ice cream ingredients, ice, and salt. Homemade ice cream never tasted so good!

If a barbeque hits the spot, but you won't be on your back patio, simply take along a portable grill or use a park that has grills and barbeque to your heart's content.

orange stick fondue

8 tablespoons butter or margarine
8 ounces sweet baking chocolate, chopped
4 tablespoons fresh orange juice
2 teaspoons fresh orange rind, grated
Variety of fresh fruits, cubed
Pound cake, cubed

1. Place butter and chocolate in fondue pot. Stir at frequent intervals until melted.

2. Stir orange juice and rind into melted chocolate mixture.

3. Dip fruit chunks and pound cake into sauce.

Note: Sauce can be prepared up to five days in advance. If prepared in advance, reheat sauce in fondue pot.

Yield: 8 servings

You have probably heard famous chefs remark that how the food is served and how the food looks is equally as important as how the food actually tastes. Along those lines, serving picnic food in unique and beautiful ways elevates the overall appeal of the picnic. As shown in the photograph above, mouth-watering Cornish game hens and roasted potatoes are served on a bed of fresh herbs in a shallow basket. It captures the senses of sight and smell as well as the sense of taste.

Make certain that whatever you choose to pose as a "serving dish" is food-safe. Sometimes, baskets or pottery use stains or materials that render food poisonous. If unsure, it's best not to use it; and it's always a good idea to provide ample separation between "dish" and food with a sanitary layer.

more
thanONE use

Veering away from traditional picnic spreads, people who are blessed with extraordinary creativity will rise to the occasion. Vibrantly colored and patterned, the picnic pictured at the left is certain to turn some heads and provoke light conversation. The hostess paid extra attention to each and every detail, and the outcome is extremely daring, spirited, and winsome.

Polka-dotted, floral, and solid-colored dishes dance merrily with plaid linens. A striped ribbon is tied around a serving spoon. Beaded ponytail holders hug candleholders, which are actually bathroom tumblers turned topsy-turvy. Black-dotted garden gloves paired with fanned plaid napkins are tucked into napkin rings, which are then tucked into mugs.

A cola glass is hot-glued to a ceramic platter, making a whimsical display of the powdered sugar cookies and the lime wedges. Hot-glue guns are fabulous because you can glue ceramics together for a special occasion and then take them apart again when the occasion is over.

All of these details collide, keeping the eyes entertained and alert. Nothing is exactly as it seems. No doubt, with a table as vibrant as this one, the picnic will be highly enjoyable and memorable.

Submarine sandwiches (above) are taken out of the cooler and served poolside from a child's sand pail. Mold flavored gelatin in sand molds to be served with the sandwiches.

I know people who use wooden clothespins to securely close bags of chips or cookies. The same sort of idea is used here, where something might have two or more uses. Fish napkin holders are slipped over large hair clips to secure a picnic tablecloth. Both adorable and functional, these clips are performing a new job.

Almost everything can be used for something else. Try taking a new pair of children's cut-off jeans and use them to hold a coffee pot filled with flowers or as a cover for a warm casserole. When you are finished using with them as a picnic accessory, they can still be worn by a child.

Linens

There is a vast variety of table linens to choose from for your picnic. You can go with a traditional red-and-white checkered, an off-white Victorian lace, or anything in between. Something that is not actually made to top tables, such as a rug, afghan, or sheet, can be used. Serving an elegant dinner on a table covered with the Sunday comics adds a touch of zaniness to your picnic.

In fact, you can even make your own table topper by following the Fitted Table Topper instructions at the right. The advantages to a home-crafted table cover is that it can be customized to fit your favorite picnic table. This table topper fits snugly over the edges of the table, making it difficult for a breeze to blow it off. It looks great alone or as a linen cover over a luxurious lace tablecloth, as shown in the photograph at the left.

The fabric you select—the patterns, colors, textures—will give the fitted table topper your creative signature. Choose deep, warm colors for an autumn feel, or lively colors with beads in lieu of the lace for a whimsical twist.

Perhaps you have more than one size of table you like to use. The Custom Tablecloth on page 40 could be made to fit the largest, allowing it to fit the others as well.

FITTED TABLE TOPPER

Materials and Supplies:
   Fabric
   Fabric scissors
   Iron and ironing board
   Lace trim
   Sewing machine
   Straight pins
   Tape measure
   Thread

Instructions:

1. Using tape measure, measure tabletop and add an additional 20" to length and width. Cut or tear fabric to these dimensions.

2. Lay fabric over table with right side down. Allow fabric to drape evenly on all sides of table.

3. Using straight pins, pin corners as shown in Illustration A.

Illustration A

4. Remove fabric from table and using sewing machine, stitch seams along pin lines. Trim excess fabric, leaving ¾" seam allowances.

5. Turn fabric right side out. Place on table to check fit and make any necessary adjustments.

6. Fold hem under ½" twice. Using iron, press in place. Pin lace onto back side of hem.

7. Stitch hem and lace in place.

A picnic is wherever you want it to be. It can be as elaborate as a sit-down dinner in a manicured garden or it can be in the back of a pick-up truck while on the road. What makes a meal a picnic is the "way" in which it is served and the little extras that make it special. A custom-made tablecloth to fit the fold-out table you carry in the back of your truck can be easily carried at all times with the emergency road kit.

Above: A custom tablecloth can be made to fit any size table, even a small one that attaches to the back of a truck via the trailer hitch.

CUSTOM TABLECLOTH

Materials and Supplies:
  Fabric scissors
  Fabrics: (2) coordinating
  Iron and ironing board
  Sewing machine
  Sewing needle
  Straight pins
  Tape measure
  Thread

Instructions:

1. Using tape measure, measure tabletop and cut or tear fabric to desired dimensions. Note: Allow enough fabric for tablecloth to drape over table edge.

2. Cut or tear two strips, at least 4" wide, from contrasting fabric to same dimension as width of tablecloth. Using sewing machine, stitch fabric strips as shown in Illustration A.

Illustration A

3. Cut or tear two strips from fabric to length of tablecloth plus 8" and stitch in place as shown in Illustration B.

Illustration B

4. Using iron, press seams toward outside edges. Fold hem under ½" and press in place. Fold pressed edge under to seam and press.

5. Fold corners to point as shown in Illustration C. Using straight pins, pin then stitch in place. Trim off excess fabric. Turn right side out and press.

Illustration C

6. Hand-stitch hem in place as shown in Illustration D.

Illustration D

Make certain to remember to add fabric napkins that can be folded and used to hold vintage silverware. These also can become an essential part of your roadside emergency kit.

Above: *This folded napkin is attractive as well as functional. After the napkin is folded, the silverware is placed inside the pouch and secured with a piece of lace, ribbon, or raffia.*

FOLDED NAPKIN SILVERWARE POCKET

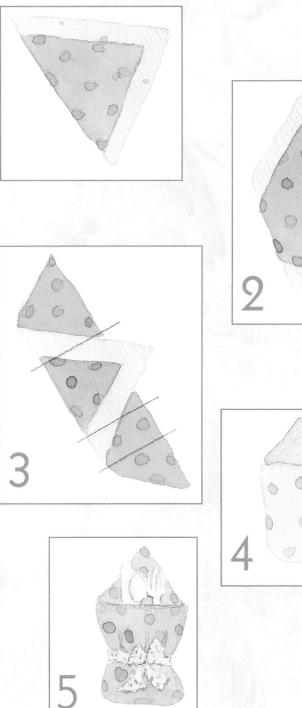

PLATE HOLDER POCKET

Materials and Supplies: (for two or three 10" plates)
    Fabrics: (2) coordinating 12" x 44"
    Sewing machine
    Sewing needle
    Straight pins
    Thread

Instructions:

1. Using sewing machine, stitch fabric pieces with right sides together, leaving an opening for turning.

2. Turn fabric right side out. Using needle and thread, stitch opening closed.

3. Fold fabric in half to find center. Open, then fold ends to center as shown in Illustration A.

Illustration A

4. Fold fabric in half with folded ends on top and bottom. Using sewing machine, stitch sides of pockets as shown in Illustration B.

Illustration B

Optional: Pockets can be added to the outside of the plate holder for napkins and silverware as shown in lower right photograph. Add an additional 6" to bottom of plate holder and fold up extra fabric before stitching sides.

Upper right: Home-crafted, purchased, or vintage linens can be used for packing breakables as well as table coverings. Lower right: Plate, glass, and wine pockets are easy to make from leftover scraps. They protect as well as help dishes to stay clean until it is time to use them.

Left: *These wine bottle and glass holder pockets are a great way to transport items made of glass. They help keep the glass items clean and protect them from being broken when traveling to the perfect picnic spot.*

WINE BOTTLE & GLASS HOLDER POCKET

Materials and Supplies:
  Fabric tape measure
  Fabrics: (2) coordinating
  Sewing machine
  Sewing needle
  Straight pins
  Thread
  Velcro®

Instructions:

  1. Using tape measure, measure height and circumference of container. Add 6" to height of container. Divide circumference by 2 and add 1½".

  2. Cut one piece from each fabric to dimensions in Step 1 for each container.

  3. Using sewing machine, stitch fabric pieces with right sides together, leaving an opening for turning.

  4. Turn fabric right side out. Using needle and thread, stitch opening closed.

  5. Fold one end of fabric up, leaving 4" flap as shown in Illustration A. Using sewing machine, stitch down each side.

  6. Stitch Velcro to flap and complementing edge of holder.

Illustration A

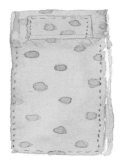

Illustration B

for a PICNIC

Picnics are a tradition that is familiar to everyone during each season in every country in the world. I am not certain if the first "official" picnic was ever documented because it seems they have existed since the beginning of time. Very early on they were simply times when meals were eaten out-of-doors while on the road traveling from one place or town to the next. However, in today's world of hectic times and crowded places, they are a retreat from the ordinary. They can be a special time to share with friends, family members, or a lover. A picnic can be a quiet time by yourself, having lunch in the park and watching the children play, or sitting by a clear stream reading a favorite novel on an autumn afternoon.

Picnics can serve any menu, be located almost anyplace, enjoyed anytime, and shared with anyone. Do not trap yourself into thinking that a picnic must be in your own backyard with everyone invited bringing potluck; up the canyon with hamburgers, hot dogs, and potato salad; by the beach on a towel with sandwiches and beer; or in the country with fried chicken served on red checked tablecloth; and . . . only when the weather is good. When planning a picnic, use your imagination and change any meal into a picnic.

On an early day in spring, sit in the rainunder a large umbrella and enjoy your lunch while the raindrops clear the air. On a snowy day in January, pack a lunch and head into the woods. Or if you don't cross-country ski, set up a table on your patio, light a fire in barbecue pit, and enjoy the fresh cold air as you appreciate a thermos of chicken noodle soup. During a busy day at the office, take a break and have a good lunch. A picnic can help you eat a little slower and actually enjoy yourself and help you forget work . . . just for a minute. It doesn't matter what the meal is or where it is; because if each is considered a picnic, you can go anywhere, include everyone, and serve the unexpected on the untraditional. Such an event can be a simple moment in time that is worth remembering or be so unforgettable that it becomes a tradition.

*P*ut your heart, mind, spirit, and soul into even your smallest acts . . . this is the secret of success.

selecting a *Site*

A glorious day with the sun shining brightly on a grassy slope next to a babbling brook provides a setting for a splendid picnic. We enlisted the help of our guests to carry the folding table, chairs, and food in baskets to this beautiful spot. The setting was next to a hiking and running trail, which meant a number of envious onlookers, including two wonderful old basset hounds. The scene was perfect for taking photos of our guests, observing the lovely shadows and sparkles on the water, and enjoying a midmorning picnic before the summer day became too warm.

Include local specialties

Incorporating the bounty of the land into your menu is a wonderful way to make your picnic memorable. For instance, people living on the Oregon coast can have a basket of freshly picked blueberries as part of the picnic spread. Those in Georgia might want to have fresh peaches for dessert, and people on the east coast can steam their seafood right on the beach. When in Florida, have a breakfast picnic complete with fresh-squeezed orange juice and a grapefruit half. If touring the California vineyards by bicycle, why not pack some cheese, crackers, and a bottle of newly discovered wine, and enjoy it beneath a roadside tree?

take a
detour

A detour off the highway and down a simple dirt road leads us to this restoring atmosphere for rest and refreshment. Unpacking a picnic basket full of china and sparkling glassware, we refresh with crisp green grapes and creamy local cheeses from our last stop. For an elaborate, yet carefree feast, stop by your favorite delicatessen and collect a sampling of exotic picnic food, or grab a take-out pizza and head for the hills. The view is splendid, and the sound of birds chirping makes refreshments even more enjoyable.

in the Woods

Although a little more thought and time is involved, few people would turn down a picnic in the woods. Being surrounded by nature has a certain magic to it—an orchestra of sights, sounds, and smells that frees the soul and delights the heart. A picnic in a forest is a beautiful way to share a meal with those you love, whether a parent, dear friend, family, or lover.

When I am on the road, I always take mental notes of places I admire and feel will be a perfect picnic site in the future. A picnic site where the soul will be nourished as well by the trilling of birds, the sound of a babbling brook, or the rustling of leaves in the breeze.

A picnic held in a woodland setting seems a bit more precious in the Autumn. This is a time when each golden leaf glows in the October light as if painted with a delicate brush by a master painter. The golden setting provides one with an atmosphere just right for savoring precious time with those people who are special in our lives—a time to celebrate the changing of the season, and reflect on the events we have shared throughout the summer.

Perhaps you simply want to grasp the last warm days of the season to bask in warmth and sunshine before winter arrives. However, whatever your desires may be—eating your food outside will enhance the senses of smell, and taste.

Finding a picnic site nearer to the road enables one to take along a few extra comforts such as a folding table, comfortable chairs, and perhaps an umbrella for shade. Take along a special tablecloth with matching napkins, pretty china, and silverware to give your picnic that little extra touch of panache. Food can be prepared ahead of time or you can simply stop by your favorite delicatessen.

The decorating, mood, and atmosphere have already been attended to by Mother Nature. Enjoy the food, the sounds, and the sunset. You may opt for leaving nature as untouched as possible for your picnic in the woods, bringing a blanket and straw basket with the basic picnic items. Or, bring spirited decorations—such as a painting propped up against a tree or a "changing tent" as pictured on the opposite page—to add a pinch of whimsy to the woodland picnic.

You can set up a picnic in the woods and then go back and gather your guests. That way, you can dazzle your guests with the picturesque picnic scene you've created just for them. To keep the magic alive, stroll through the forest with your guests when everyone has finished eating, and enjoy the atmosphere, leaving the cleanup for later on.

along the water's edge

There's something about a body of water, whether a backyard swimming pool or Niagara Falls, that puts people in a state of awe. That's why picnicking close to water is such a refreshing idea. It can be playful and spontaneous, like the beach and a bucket of fried chicken, or romantic, like a deli takeout beside a cascading waterfall. For a breezy, hair-tousled, romantic time, organize a sailing picnic for the one you love. Whether a cooler of snacks or a basket complete with appetizer, main course, and dessert, sharing a romantic meal is a terrific way to make a picnic extra special.

Mother Nature radiates in a setting composed of a gently flowing river, sprinkles from waterfalls, majestic trees, and rainbow-splashed rocks. If you choose a setting such as this for your next picnic, be forewarned that you will need to take time to soak in the splendor of the atmosphere. Eat slowly, marveling at the taste and smell—for this picnic just might be etched in your senses forever.

on the trail

Have you ever noticed how delicious food tastes when you are camping? All of your senses are on alert—and it's times like these that a hot dog roasted over an open fire tastes better than the filet mignon you ate at a steakhouse last week. When you're camping, every meal is a picnic. Sometimes on a picnic table, other times on a blanket in the wilderness or perched on a log by the camp fire. You can enjoy a picnic on a Sunday afternoon hike or for weeks on end at a favorite campsite.

The food you eat will be determined by how long you're out in the wilderness, as well as how far out you go. If you're on a month-long backpacking trip, you'll pack food that is light in weight and won't spoil. On the other hand, if you're just going for a one-hour hike, you can pack all the "fixin's" in your backpack. Some department and sporting goods stores sell backpacks that are designed especially for picnicking, including the utensils, plates, cups, tablecloth—even wine bottle openers and cheese boards. All you have to do is add the food, and make certain all the lids are on tightly!

on-the-trail Coney dogs

¼ pound lean hamburger
6 ounces tomato paste
1½ cups water
¼ cup pickle relish
2 tablespoons onion, finely chopped
1 tablespoon prepared mustard
3 teaspoons chili powder
1 teaspoon sugar
8 hot dogs, grilled
8 hot dog buns, toasted on grill

1. Brown hamburger and drain well. Mix hamburger and all ingredients, except hot dogs and buns, together. Simmer for 30 minutes.

2. Place hot dogs in buns and top with mixture.

Yield: 8 servings

Left: *Remember the aluminum foil and Dutch ovens for cooking over hot coals while on the trail. Enjoy camp fire stories and legends while slowly cooking a hearty feast of chicken, baked potatoes, and corn.*

for a **crowd**

Above: Select an area where there is plenty of seating and a fire pit for swapping tales and socializing. **Left:** Select a location that is accommodating to all who will be participating, such as any elderly and children. **Opposite page, upper left:** Decorate the table with centerpieces that can double as door prizes or favors, such as these potted herbs and darling flowerpots. **Opposite page, lower left:** Allow guests to bring a favored potluck dish from home, such as a homemade barbeque sauce that is their personal trademark. **Opposite page, right:** Place signs or mark drink containers so that guests can quickly and easily select a beverage.

When preparing a picnic for a crowd, it's best to serve food that can be made ahead of time or grilled while the guests are arriving. Include hot dogs, hamburgers or other child-friendly menu items if children are coming.

A potluck picnic is especially convenient and effective when there will be a lot of people coming. Plus, when everyone brings a dish, it adds a delightful myriad of different tastes and presentations.

A few things to keep in mind when having a picnic for a crowd are:

❧ Use disposable dishes, cups, and utensils so you don't have to worry about dishes afterwards.

❧ Set up the food buffet-style, allowing each guest to fill their plate as desired. Set up a drink station close to the buffet line.

❧ Supply the drink station with cups, ice, and coolers or jugs of soda pop, lemonade or punch, iced tea, and water.

POTLUCKING IT

❧ Have each guest bring a food item that corresponds with the first letter of their last name, (i.e. A–F Appetizers, G–L Salads, M–R Main Dish*, S–Z Desserts.)
*The Robinsons brought the ribs.

❧ Have each guest bring a dish representing their heritage.

When the weather cooperates, having a large-scale picnic is a great way to feed a crowd. Try organizing a picnic for your next family reunion, church function, friends and their families, or neighborhood gathering. If your backyard isn't spacious enough, many public parks have covered picnic table areas that can be reserved. Make certain to bring plenty of tablecloths—whether linen, plastic, or paper—to cover the tables and make a more sanitary eating environment.

in the Garden

There's nothing quite as enchanting as a picnic in a beautiful garden. Plus, it is a great way to showcase the floral and shrubbery masterpieces into which you've put so much thought and effort. A garden picnic is a perfect way to thank your best friend for being there for you, for sharing in laughter and tears, and for being such a wonderful person. Your family will enjoy a picnic in the garden because they will get all of the good food and picturesque scenery without having to take hours out of their busy schedules.

If you do not have a table in your garden, simply spread a couple of colorful quilts on the freshly trimmed grass. Find a place that is relatively flat and surrounded with beautiful flowers. If statues or other decorative structures adorn your garden, setting up your picnic with those in view adds a nice touch.

Pack the food in a wicker basket, remembering the vegetables you picked from your garden that morning. Your menu should be fresh and colorful, like the garden itself. If your lady friends are the guests, spinach quiche is simply divine. For a family affair, slices of granny smith apples and chicken salad stuffed into whole-wheat pitas makes a tantalizing and easy main dish.

While your house might only be a few feet away, try to remember everything you need for the picnic so the tenderness of the occasion isn't interrupted by your running back to the kitchen for forgotten items. And while music playing in the background is a wonderful mood-enhancer for some types of picnics, it's best for Mother Nature to be the musician for a garden picnic. You won't want Mozart or a collection of party tunes covering up the splendid song of the red robin, singing from her nest, or the sounds of nature.

If you decide to host a garden picnic, you might even send the guests home with "party favors" picked from your garden. A basket of strawberries, a bunch of fresh mint sprigs tied together with ribbon, a couple of zucchinis or tomatoes, an assortment of herbs, a bouquet of yellow roses—anything that will entice the senses and remind the guests what a nice time they had at your picnic.

A garden is the masterpiece painted by Mother Nature, framed by the gardener. And while not everybody has a green thumb, most people enjoy being garden spectators—experiencing the pathways, birdbaths, pruned bushes, flowerbeds, rows of vegetables, and everything else that makes a garden such a magical place.

Even if you don't have your own garden, you can still enjoy the beauty of a garden picnic. Most likely, you can find a public garden in your town. Some are tucked away—secluded and quaint. Others are rather large, complete with paddleboats, nature hikes, and paved pathways. If you picnic in a public garden, be extra sensitive to instated rules, make certain you leave no trace of your visit, and do not feed the wildlife unless it is permitted.

Whether it's deep in a forest or on your back lawn, one of the most beloved traits of a picnic is indulging your taste buds while marveling at the great outdoors. What better way to celebrate life than to phone a dear neighbor and invite her over for lemon iced shortbread cookies and lemonade in your backyard? It's the perfect setting for a heartfelt tête-à-tête, and you'll be thankful for each other and for the beautiful day.

For a more casual feel, you can use disposable dishes and utensils in pretty patterns and whimsical color combinations. Or, mix and match the traditional red-and-white plaid picnic ensemble with floral patterned dishes. For fun, serve citrus punch in plastic champagne flutes. If it's a particularly hot day, perch open beach umbrellas or regular umbrellas around the picnic spot—a festive decoration that doubles as a welcome shade-maker.

Little details can add instant refreshment to a dull, hot summer day. Decorate patio furniture with delicate white linens and a bouquet of flowers picked from your garden. Bring out the silver tea set and platter that is tucked back in your china cabinet for a tea party on your front porch. To add a touch of elegance, scatter flower heads randomly over the picnic blanket. When you take a moment to make special touches, your picnic—whether casual or fancy—becomes a memorable and delightful occasion.

frosted lemon shortbread cookies

1 cup butter	Frosting:
½ cup powdered sugar	¼ cup butter, melted
⅔ cup cornstarch	2 tablespoons lemon juice
1 cup flour	Rind of one lemon, grated
	2½–3 cups powered sugar

1. Cream butter and sugar. Stir in cornstarch and flour.

2. Drop by teaspoonfuls on a cookie sheet.

3. Bake at 325° for 15 minutes. Cool.

4. Combine frosting ingredients. Spread on cooled cookies.

Yield: 2½ dozen cookies

fresh lemonade

2 cups lemon juice
4 cups sugar
2 cups water
6 lemon rinds, pared in strips
2–3 bottles club soda
Fresh mint

1. Squeeze lemons to get 2 cups. Set aside.

2. Dissolve sugar in water over low heat. Add lemon rind.

3. Bring to boil. Simmer for 5 minutes. Cool. Add lemon juice. Cover. Refrigerate.

4. To serve, strain, and dilute with club soda to desired taste. Garnish with mint leaves.

Yield: 10 servings

Why not spread out a pretty cloth or scarf and enjoy a good bottle of wine with crusty bread, Brie cheese, and fresh fruit on a rustic porch swing in the early spring? A refreshing breeze and a few early blossoms share this special occasion. As you gently sway back and forth, conversation naturally turns to rejuvenation of the spirit, the beauty of the world you live in, and your growing fondness of each other.

For a more casual air, a swing picnic is a wonderful way to celebrate the first day of summer vacation with your children. After an entire year of eating lunches in the school cafeteria, eating homemade peanut butter cookies and sipping cold milk on a porch swing is a welcome change. A porch swing picnic is a great time to catch up, share secrets, and discuss upcoming summer plans together.

homemade ice cream

2⅔ cups sugar
1 quart whole milk
5 ounces evaporated milk
3 cups heavy cream
3 cups fresh ripe peaches, peeled, pureed
½ cup pineapple juice
Juice of 2 oranges
Lemon juice to taste
Ice
Rock salt

1. Dissolve sugar in whole milk in the container of a 6-quart ice cream freezer. Using long wooden spoon, stir mixture several times to completely dissolve sugar.

2. Add evaporated milk and heavy cream. Stir to mix. Refrigerate cream mixture while preparing fruit juice.

3. Mix pureed peaches and juices together.

4. Add juice mixture to cream mixture. Stir well to blend. Freeze according to manufacturer's freezing instructions.

Yield: 8–10 servings

The very mention of a picnic conjures up old-fashioned images—sweet memories of how life was so charming, families were so close, and hard work was rewarded with home-cooked goodies. Yesterday has come and gone, yet we can still attempt to capture the essence by re-creating that which we still cherish and long for in our lives today.

Instead of an electric ice cream freezer, use an old one that must be hand-cranked for authentic old-fashioned homemade ice cream. As pictured on the upper left, fresh peaches can be mixed into homemade vanilla ice cream for a sweet and creamy taste of heaven. Whether eaten as a picnic snack—alone or as a sidekick to a freshly baked fruit pie—or as a dessert following a picnic supper, the extra work put into creating this special ice cream will be noticed and appreciated by all.

Besides including an old-fashioned menu item in your picnic, you can add wholesome charm by incorporating old-fashioned accessories. As seen in the photograph on the opposite page, a pair of old washtubs found at a flea market were painted and instantly transformed into endearing containers for chilled drinks and ice. Both functional and decorative, these tubs bring a breath of nostalgia to the picnic scene.

theme picnic

While picking fruit from your garden orchard, have a theme picnic, such as the cherries theme, pictured here. Cherries symbolize youth, happiness, and warmer days to come. Tablecloths trimmed in cherry patterns and cherry-stenciled dishes adorn the table. A basket of freshly picked cherries is both the centerpiece and a tasty part of the picnic menu. Even a cherry-picking ladder leans comfortably against a nearby tree, creating a charming backdrop for the picnic scene. Every little detail comes together nicely to produce a temporary cherry land. Other ideas derived from nature include a fall pumpkin theme, or butterflies, ladybugs, or birds for spring or summertime.

When coming up with picnic theme ideas, consider color combinations. If the picnic is by the sea, how about using green and blue tones to dress the table? A black-and-white color theme would be spectacular in a colorful garden setting. Picnic themes based around national or local holidays show off your community spirit.

If you or your guests have a certain hobby or interest, incorporate that into the picnic theme. For instance, if your children are little artists, have them decorate a paper tablecloth and paper plates and cups with paint or markers. If you collect porcelain dolls, why not have a tea party picnic, using your dolls as decorations?

A theme picnic is a great way to spotlight something from nature or something about yourself or your guests. Inspiration is all around you, and with a little creativity and attention to detail, the outcome will be a picnic as fresh as the basket of cherries.

71

COUNTRY garden *picnic*

One warm summer day while my husband and I were working in the garden on our New England farm, our bodies needed a break. I set out bread, Kasseri cheese, prosciutto ham, vegetables, and fruit from the garden for a quick, yet nourishing snack. The snack lunch was transported from house to yard in a small garden cart. I covered small potting tables with tablecloths, on which the food and a bottle of chilled champagne—left over from a summer wedding—were placed. As we experienced this impromptu picnic, we realized how lucky we were to live in this beautiful area and to be able to spend special times like these together.

backyard picnic

On a summer evening, I find that turning the oven on makes our house too hot. So, instead of baking chicken, I simply turn on the outdoor grill for an impromptu garden barbeque picnic. It's amazing how many things can be prepared on a grill—garlic bread, pineapple, corn on the cob, even apple crisp!

If you have a Dutch oven, you can create a variety of culinary masterpieces outside. Even if you prepare all the food in your kitchen, taking it out-doors to eat it makes the meal more enjoyable. All in all, most meals can be served outdoors as easily as indoors. And in many cases, those few extra steps to carry the food outside are worthwhile.

grilled corn in the husks

8 ears of corn
Flavored butter
Cotton string

1. Pull husks back from corn. Remove and discard silk.

2. Brush or spread 1 tablespoon flavored butter over each ear of corn.

3. Pull husks up to cover corn. Tie husk ends together with water-soaked string.

4. Place corn on grill and cook for 12–15 minutes, regularly rotating corn to make certain it does not burn.

Yield: 8 servings

flavored butters

Santa Fe chipotle butter

1 chipotle chili in adobo sauce
¾ cup butter
1 clove garlic, minced
¼ teaspoon ground cumin
½ teaspoon salt

1. Puree chili in blender or food processor until smooth.

2. Melt butter in small saucepan with 1½ teaspoons chipotle puree, garlic, cumin, and salt over low heat.

Yield: 8 servings

herb garden & spice butter

¾ cup butter, softened
1½ tablespoons fresh lemon juice
¼ teaspoon freshly grated nutmeg
1½ tablespoons freshly minced parsley
2½ tablespoons freshly minced green onion
¼ teaspoon Worcestershire sauce

1. Blend all ingredients together and refrigerate for one hour, allowing flavors to mingle.

Yield: 8 servings

hearty pumpkin soup

1 tablespoon butter
1 tablespoon flour
3 cups pumpkin, canned or fresh, cooked
3 cups scalded milk or chicken broth
2 tablespoons brown sugar
Salt and pepper to taste
½ cup ham, chopped
Ginger (optional)
Cinnamon (optional)
½ cup sliced almonds
¾ cup cream (if using chicken broth)
Sour cream (optional)
Parmesan (optional)
Mint leaves (optional)

1. Melt butter in large saucepan and stir in flour.

2. Blend pumpkin and milk or broth into butter and flour mixture.

3. Add brown sugar, salt, pepper, ham, ginger, cinnamon, and light cream (if broth was used). Continue stirring over medium heat until mixture is hot, but not boiling. Add almonds to soup.

4. Place in soup bowls and garnish with sour cream, parmesan cheese, and mint leaves as desired.

Yield: 6–8 servings

Autumn fare

The garden is still enjoyable on a crisp October day. A round table positioned underneath the rose arbor and dressed in a woolen blanket and oriental rug set the scene nicely. Lovely brown transfer dishes accent the table, while warmly colored flowers and pumpkins from the garden add color and theme. A hearty soup such as pumpkin soup tastes heavenly when eaten on a nippy autumn afternoon. Hot cider or hot tea keeps shivers at bay, and gingerbread or a spice cake hits the spot for dessert.

Many folks would agree that autumn is the loveliest of all seasons, so it's only natural to want to be outdoors when the weather is pleasantly chilly and the bronze and orange leaves sway back and forth on the limbs. The garden is perfect on a beautiful fall day, with the autumn crop ready for harvest and the last eggplant-hued flowers standing tall and relentless for a few more precious days.

Autumn is a fabulous season to host a garden picnic. While the color schemes and menu items are warmer than a typical spring or summertime picnic, with a little thought and consideration, your sweater-clad guests will certainly appreciate being a part of your picnic party.

on the Porch

Less traditional than a picnic table or a blanket spread in the park, a picnic served on the porch is a popular favorite of people everywhere. In fact, some areas that are prone to insects have screened-in porches for the purpose of dining outdoors without having to share the food with an unwelcome pest. Picnics can be served on the back porch, front porch, patio, deck, balcony, or along a southern-style wraparound porch. Some apartments have access to rooftop areas that can set the scene for a passionate picnic with a beau, especially at night. Or, if the best scenery from your porch is the neighbor's living room, consider having a picnic on the porch next time you rent a condo or cabin while on a vacation.

A porch picnic can be at any time of day, and for any meal or a quick snack. What better way to start the day than eating breakfast on the front porch? Or, host a Sunday afternoon barbeque from your back deck. Strings of tiny lights strung through the rails of a balcony make a lovely backdrop for a romantic dinner.

Since your house is usually not too far from your porch, serving a porch picnic is easier than taking a picnic in a backpack on a hike in the mountains. For this reason, you might choose to use china, silverware, and fine linen napkins in lieu of disposable ones. The bread can be served hot and fresh, right out of the oven. Use the convenience factor to your favor.

If your porch is wide enough, consider using a table (even a card table disguised with a pretty linen tablecloth) for your picnic. If your porch is too narrow for a table, space out chairs so each guest has enough elbow room, yet is close enough and angled such that everyone can be seen and heard. The guests can simply hold their plates in their laps and set their drinks beside their chairs; or, better yet, you can set baskets, scarf-topped TV trays, or any other makeshift table in front of each chair.

springtime
buffet

It's springtime and the flowers open in a rainbow of splendor. Baby birds chirp from their nest, and a revitalizing breeze puffs through the budding leaves. Wispy clouds speckle the bright blue sky, What a spectacular day for a picnic.

A plate of sandwiches, those famous sugar cookies, and a pitcher of homemade lemonade make a splendid spread for a birthday party or a circle-of-friends get-together. The food is served in individual portions and the guests help themselves, buffet-style.

White lace linens cloak the tables, and a vase of pristine flowers stands tall as the centerpiece. Crystal glasses and crisp white plates are simple, yet not humble. These added touches lend elegance to the picnic, suitable for intimate gatherings.

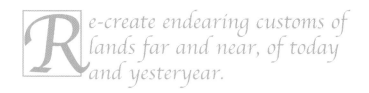
*R*e-create endearing customs of lands far and near, of today and yesteryear.

Above: *An oversized chocolate muffin in a coffee basket filter served with fresh strawberries is a tasty treat for a porch picnic.* **Left:** *Tiny finger sandwiches can be made the traditional way with white or wheat bread and cut into tiny triangles; or they can be made from unusual breads such as pimento-parmesan and cut into cookie-cutter shapes. Have the breads "flavor" the occasion, then they are a picnic touch that is very special indeed.*

Morning air

Enjoying a picnic on the porch is a wonderful way to start the day. Whether a leisurely Sunday brunch or a quick weekday breakfast, fresh air and good food is a winning combination. Pictured above, French toast blanketed in a medley of fresh berries makes a tasty picnic treat. Blueberry pancakes and maple syrup, as pictured to the right, makes a grand entrance with potted primroses in a flat basket.

European pleasures

If you are fortunate enough to travel the world, there is no doubt you have noticed the rainbow of traditions different countries and towns hold dear.

An atmosphere that is especially pleasing to re-create is that found in an Italian villa. A lovely table, dressed in crisp white linens and topped with the finest china sets the mood. Food items and decorations harvested from an ethnic market, such as the European lemonade in the photograph above, instates authenticity. As is tradition in fine European restaurants, a fresh fruit or sorbet is served in crystal bowls to prepare the pallet for the delectable meal to come.

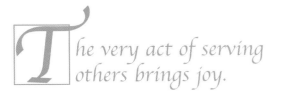

The very act of serving others brings joy.

A timeless medley of Italian love songs escapes from the open living-room window as pasta prepared with fresh garden vegetables and olive oil, crusty Italian bread, and red wine are enjoyed. As the last bite of Tiramisu is relished and the café au lait is sipped, this type of porch picnic is certain to be remembered for quite some time.

You can also have a porch picnic with a historical theme, such as Victorian. Dress the table in white lacy linens and use your finest place settings and tea set. You can even go as far as dressing the part, donning the Victorian hat you found in an antique shop in New Hampshire last year.

These are just a few examples of the endless possibilities to make your picnic on the porch unique and memorable. The convenience of having the kitchen nearby and the potential of remarkable views makes having porch picnics fun and invigorating.

provencal pasta

¼ cup olive oil
4 garlic cloves, peeled
1 medium zucchini, cut into thin matchsticks
1 medium yellow Italian squash, cut into thin matchsticks
1 medium carrot, cut into thin strips
Salt
¼ pound linguini
¾ cup basil, coarsely chopped
1 cup parmesan cheese, freshly grated
Pepper

1. Preheat the oven to 375°. In a baking dish, combine olive oil and garlic cloves. Bake for 10–15 minutes or until garlic is golden. Remove from oven and using slotted spoon, discard garlic.

2. Add zucchini, yellow squash, and carrots to oil. Toss well. Return to oven. Bake for 10 minutes or until vegetables are slightly softened.

3. Meanwhile, in a large pot of boiling salted water, cook linguini for 6 minutes or until al dente. Drain linguini and add to vegetable mixture.

4. Add basil, salt, pepper, and ½ cup of parmesan cheese. Toss well. Season with salt and pepper to taste. Serve warm or at room temperature. Top with remaining parmesan cheese.

Yield: 4 servings

chapter seven

in
unusual
Places

A picnic doesn't have to be on a picnic table in the park. Use your imagination to discover extra-special and unexpected places to hold a picnic. Having a picnic in an unusual spot is an easy and certain way to add panache to your next picnic.

Why not host a picnic in the parking lot—off the back of your car or truck? What a unique dinner after taking your date to the movies! Or, how about lunch at a construction site? As shown in the photograph on the opposite page, a sheepherder's camp makes quite a unique setting for a picnic. A sheet-covered card table is set with pretty dishes and a delicious picnic is waiting in the basket. In late October, a cornfield sets the stage for a hauntingly unusual picnic. Having lunch in a barn—complete with horses nudging the barn door, begging for a handful of oats—is a creative picnic place sure to delight adults and children alike. Transform a bail of hay into a table by covering it with a tablecloth and enjoy!

As long as there is no perceived danger and you have permission to dine on someone else's property, you can picnic almost anywhere. However, you will want to take into consideration the personalities and any health restrictions of your guests. You won't want to take Great Aunt Beatrice to the top of a waterfall for a picnic if she uses a wheelchair and is afraid of heights or water. For a rule of thumb, make certain the picnic destination is comfortable enough for everybody so that they can relax and enjoy the meal.

After you have taken the time to find an ideally creative place for your picnic, don't forget to keep the picnic itself special. The simple touches, such as a basket of potted violets centered on a fold-out table, will make the most imaginative picnics especially memorable. You can go with the theme of the picnic site, such as serving barbeque in a barn on hay-bail tables; or choose to contradict the theme such as serving a gourmet meal on fine china at a sheepherder's camp.

in greenhouse
the

A picnic can serve as a thank you or as a way to let someone know that they are special and you enjoy spending time with them.

I have a special friend who owns a greenhouse and calls me when special plants come in, or takes my dying plants and nurses them back to health. Because of this, I wanted to do something special for him, so I planned a special lunch setting in the middle of his greenhouse. I picked a day of the week when business was slower and showed up at the greenhouse with a table, chairs, dishes, chopsticks, and other picnic paraphernalia. I picked up a full-course Chinese meal, complete with fortune cookies and Jasmine tea,

*When friends meet,
hearts are warmed.*

from a local Chinese restaurant. The setting was extraordinary as we dined among exotic plants that included orchids, lilies, and orange trees. This special picnic made memories that will never be forgotten.

on _the_ rooftop

The rooftop adds an exciting dimension to a picnic with friends and family. Some apartments have flat rooftops from which the view is outstanding, with lavish mini gardens, a dining table, and chairs. A rooftop garden is the perfect setting for alfresco dining. One can enjoy the gentle breezes as well as the view. An umbrella and comfortable pillows placed on wicker chairs will make dining on the roof extra special.

If your roof is simply a bunch of shingles stapled together, yet there is a flat or semiflat portion, you can create an impressive picnic spot with some imagination, exceptional props, and a little time.

If the sun has set, light tapered candles or hang small lamps for light and atmosphere. Don't forget the music—select tunes that fit the mood or the theme of your picnic. You will find that guests tend to linger into the night at rooftop picnics, sharing conversation while stargazing.

in *a* tepee

Bring a sense of history and adventure to your next picnic by having it in a tepee. You can even blindfold the guests, march them up to the tepee one by one, and surprise them with the dining space.

Invite everyone to sit cross-legged in a big circle on the floor, then tuck feathers into everyone's hair if you want the full impact. While enjoying the home-made chili, fresh corn on the cob, and tortillas, you can almost hear the drums beating in the distance. Fry-bread sprinkled with sugar and cinnamon is a perfect dessert for your powwow picnic. After everyone has eaten, stay in the tepee and share stories of yesterday and tomorrow.

on the range

For a picnic with western flair, serve up some vittles on the outskirts of a hometown rodeo. With cowboys and cowgirls, horses, cows, rodeo clowns, and rowdy fans in the background, a picnic here is sure to be a good time!

These young cowboys say "Yippee!" when they see you drive up with breakfast in the back of your pickup truck. Hard at work early in the morning, they welcome homemade biscuits and steaming hot coffee, and a well-deserved break. The cattle look on, waiting patiently for the cowboys to finish eating.

CHUCKWAGON BREAKFAST IDEAS

❧ Previously baked potatoes, sliced, then fried with diced onions and sliced jalapeno peppers.

❧ Grilled sausage patties and toast.

❧ Eggs scrambled with chorizo sausage, topped with black-bean salsa and monterey jack cheese, then served with warm tortillas.

Any meal on the range is a big event that is anticipated long before the appointed hour. Everyone works hard and it seems that when work is completed outside in the fresh air, appetites are twice what they normally would be. So the meals whether breakfast, lunch, or dinner are hearty, ample, and oftentimes seem like a gourmet delight. Chuckwagon cooks are like the cooks at roadside cafes where the truckers stop—the food is always guaranteed to be good.

One way to surprise your ranch hands, however, might be to serve their meal from dishes on patterned cloths in wicker baskets, with a touch of wine to help with their digestion. They will appreciate any special touch that you take the time to do because it is so very unexpected and so very "not the ordinary."

Above: This appetite-satisfying lasagna can be cooked ahead of time and placed in a food warmer or immediately transported to the picnic site and served while still hot.

range lasagna

3 tablespoons olive oil
2 cloves garlic, chopped
2½ pounds ripe roma tomatoes
8 ounces tomato sauce
Salt and pepper
15 ounces ricotta cheese
½ cup parmesan cheese, grated
1 pound mozzarella cheese, grated
2 eggs, beaten
Pinch of nutmeg
16 lasagna noodles, cooked
½ cup fresh basil leaves
⅓ cup pine nuts, chopped

1. Heat olive oil in medium skillet and sauté garlic until golden.

2. Remove skins from tomatoes and combine tomatoes with tomato sauce. Puree in food processor or blender. Pour tomatoes into saucepan and season with salt and pepper. Simmer until sauce thickens, approximately 20 minutes.

3. Combine ricotta cheese, parmesan cheese, ½ of the mozzarella, egg, and nutmeg. Stir to blend well. Reserve the remaining mozzarella cheese for top of lasagna.

4. Place a thin layer of tomato mixture in bottom of 9" x 13" baking pan. Place four noodles over sauce.

5. Spread ½ of cheese mixture and ½ of the basil leaves over noodles and top with four noodles.

6. Pour ½ of remaining tomato mixture on noodles and top with four noodles. Spread remaining cheese mixture and basil leaves on noodles and top with remaining noodles.

7. Pour remaining tomato mixture on noodles. Top with pine nuts and remaining mozzarella cheese. Bake lasagna 45 minutes in 350°F preheated oven. Allow lasagna to sit for 20 minutes before serving.

Yield: 8–12 servings

** Noodles could be cooked the day before and refrigerated between layers of waxed paper.

* Lasagna could be made in a foil-lined 10" Dutch oven over coals.

Above: *Beverages can be chilled in ice in a stoneware pot.*

A picnic in the snow makes a fabulous break for wintertime sports and activities. Simply pack a basket of munchies for a quick pick-me-up while ice-skating on a frozen pond. Call the kids over for snow ice cream between snowball fights, and they might just forget which team was winning! Hand the neighborhood kids brown-bagged lunches to eat in the igloo they built in the backyard. After their picnic break, they will have the energy to create yet another snowy architectural masterpiece.

Cross-country skiing and snowshoeing in the mountains are ideal opportunities to enjoy a wintertime picnic. You are already out enjoying the splendor of the winter day—and undoubtedly, you're working up a mighty appetite.

Last January, when we were snow shoeing on a brisk, yet sunny day, we dug a hole in the snow, large enough to accommodate two, and placed cushions from our backpacks in the hole for seats. A picnic, purchased that morning from a local delicatessen, consisted of roast beef sandwiches, pumpkin pie, and frosty imported beer.

the in Snow

Having a picnic on a snowy day celebrates the winter wonderland in a new and festive spirit. If it's a mild winter day, consider having a picnic outside. Bring hot cocoa and graham crackers out on your balcony for a merry snacking experience. If you are at a ski resort, eat your lunch outside on the provided picnic tables rather than the overcrowded dining hall in the lodge.

There's nothing quite like a steamy bowl of homemade soup to warm your bones on a chilly winter day. Chicken noodle soup has long been recognized for helping people get over the common cold, even though its healing qualities have not been scientifically proven. Nevertheless, chicken noodle soup definitely warms you up and tastes great. Chicken noodle soup is a perfect main dish or supplement to a cold-weather picnic menu. Simply pour it into a thermos, take it to a picnic spot, pour it into bowls, and enjoy every warm spoonful.

simmering chicken soup

½ onion, diced
1 carrot, thinly sliced
2 stalks celery, sliced
1 cup fresh or frozen peas
2 teaspoons fresh thyme, chopped
2 tablespoons fresh parsley, chopped
7 cups chicken broth
Salt and pepper
½ pound fresh egg noodles, wide
2 precooked chicken breasts, diced or shredded
1 tomato, peeled, seeded, and diced
Fresh parsley and dill for garnish

1. Place all vegetables (except tomato), thyme, parsley, and broth in large saucepan. Season with salt and pepper to taste. Bring to a boil and simmer for 5 minutes.

2. Add noodles to vegetables and cook 5–8 minutes or until tender. Add chicken and tomato. Simmer 5 minutes and serve. Garnish with parsley and dill leaves.

Yield: 6–8 servings

on the Road

A day on the road—whether it is a leisurely Sunday drive in the mountains or the first day of a cross-country road trip with the entire family—can be extra special with a ready-made picnic lunch in the trunk. It's always nice to get out of the car, stretch your legs, and experience the scenery you are driving through, close up.

While growing up, my friend's family would drive their old van from Denver to Orlando almost every summer. Her mom was a firm believer that the journey should be savored, and while the kids were anxious to get to Disney World, they always had fun adventures during the four- to five-day road trip. They never ate their meals in the van; instead, they would stop alongside the road at scenic spots or established rest stops and have a picnic. She fondly remembers the pimento

cheese and fresh tomato on rye bread sandwiches, the crispy cheese chips, the bite-sized broccoli and cauliflower spears, the boxed fruit drinks, and the snickerdoodle cookies that were lovingly prepared before the trip. The cooler and the red-and-white plaid tablecloth were permanent fixtures in the back of the van. The special stopping places, the good food, and finally making it to Disney World etched wonderful memories in my friend's and her siblings' minds.

Because a car picnic is so versatile, you can bring the food and accessories you desire, provided everything fits in your car somehow. And since you are covering many miles in a short amount of time, you can be selective where you picnic. You can even stop by a waterfall for dinner and a lush green pasture for dessert an hour down the road.

antique road *trip*

Picnics should be a family tradition —and it may already be. It may be a tradition that has been there all the time and you just failed to realize that such a tradition had existed in your family at all. Go back through the family photo albums and see if there are pictures of your grandparents, having their own picnic. What did they serve? Where were they held? Now recreate those days that have been a part of your family for longer than you know and while you are eating have your parents tell the stories of the picnics they had with their parents.

This page and opposite page: *These vintage family photographs show that picnicking has been a pursuit enjoyed by family members of all ages for generations.*

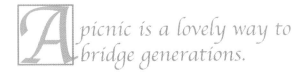

Uncle Jack's Dutch oven corn bread

4 tablespoons powdered buttermilk
1 cup water
1 cup yellow cornmeal
1 cup white flour
2 tablespoons sugar
4 teaspoons baking powder
½ teaspoon salt
1 large egg

1. In a large bowl, mix powdered buttermilk in one cup of water.

2. Add remaining ingredients to buttermilk. Stir slowly until all dry ingredients are moistened. Beat vigorously for 90 seconds.

3. Place 10" Dutch oven over a ring of hot charcoals. Pour corn bread mixture into Dutch oven. Cover with lid.

4. Place 1½ rings of hot charcoals on top of Dutch oven lid. Cook for 20–25 minutes.

Yield: 6–8 servings

103

Ocean Side

Exploring the local beaches by auto is a magnificent way to spend the day if you are lucky enough to live within driving distance of a beach. Pack some food in the trunk of your car for setting up a picnic on the sand. The sound of the tide washing up on the sand is music to your ears, and the blue water or a quaint lighthouse makes a fabulous backdrop for the occasion.

Instead of traditional sandwiches and chips, try serving seafood. If you want to save time for a volleyball game, pick up some fish and chips from a local vendor and bring it to the beach to eat. If you crave fish at its freshest, consider bringing a fishing pole to catch your main dish, or buy fish at the pier market. Cooking the seafood at the picnic site is fun and the seafood has never tasted better.

gazpacho

4 cups clam-flavored tomato juice
½ cup onion, minced
⅓ cup olive oil
⅓ cup wine vinegar
¼ cup green pepper, minced
3 tablespoons parsley, chopped
2 cloves garlic, minced
¼ teaspoon hot-pepper sauce
Salt and pepper to taste
8 tomatoes, chopped
2 cucumbers, chopped
2 avocados, cubed
Garlic croutons
Grated parmesan cheese

1. Combine tomato juice, onion, olive oil, wine vinegar, green pepper, parsley, garlic, hot-pepper sauce, salt, and pepper.

2. Refrigerate six hours or overnight.

3. Add tomatoes, cucumbers, and avocados. Refrigerate.

4. Serve very cold with croutons and parmesan cheese.

Yield: 8 servings

Above: The seaside picnic menu features gazpacho, chilled dungeness crab, steamed clams with drawn butter, baby greens salad with sweet peppers and red onion, pineapple pudding, and wine.

a tailgate
picnic

A tailgate picnic is charming in its simplicity. Park your truck just about anywhere, hop up, and enjoy a picnic on the tailgate. Homemade pot-pie—simply delicious—is an ideal dish for a tailgater. From a quick snack of beer with tortilla chips and salsa to an elegant dinner by candlelight, all you need is someone to share it with.

As shown above, you can buy and assemble a table, complete with umbrella, made especially for a tailgate picnic. A pretty tablecloth and fluffy pillows add a special touch.

❧ Always have a bag for trash on hand.

❧ For long road trips, include nonperishable foods such as dried fruit, peanut butter, crackers, and individually canned fruits or meats.

❧ Small packets of condiments are easier to travel with than the full-sized versions that will need refrigeration.

❧ A Swiss army knife is handy since it can provide a cork-screw and can opener.

Biker *Lunch*

If you are on the road and you are traveling by "bike" don't pull in to the nearest fast-food stop and stay. Get your meal to go and enjoy it at a local park. On your way, buy a small bouquet of fresh flowers to put on the table and use the flowered cloths that you carry in your pack everywhere you go. Biker's love to be on the road with all that it has to offer; so take advantage and make each and every aspect of your day on the road both delightful and memorable.

in the Home

Picnics enjoyed in the home can be just as creative and special as any held out-of-doors. Try setting up in a corner, near a window, in the bedroom, in the attic, in front of the fireplace, in an enclosed porch, the garage, and even in the kitchen. A folding table, when draped with a pretty cloth, can create an instant dining area in any space.

Fresh flowers from the garden or the market down the street instantly boost your mood, as well as the moods of anyone entering your home. Plus, flowers are a great way to bring a bit of the outdoors indoors. A lovely bouquet adds a special touch of elegance to any space in which we choose to dine. A TV tray decorated with a single red rose and cloth napkins makes a beautifully romantic setting for a picnic. The color and fragrance of flowers will stimulate your appetite, increase the flavor of the food, and add mood.

Additionally, those treasured and unusual linens, dishes, and centerpieces you have collected will set your picnic space apart from typical dining areas such as the kitchen table and dining room. With a change of perspective, every plate of food that is eaten outside of the usual dining areas becomes a festive picnic and a memorable meal.

a
Christmas
picnic

You can enhance your family's holiday traditions or introduce new traditions with a picnic indoors. Traditional events such as cutting down a Christmas tree and bringing it into the home to trim can be enhanced by enjoying an indoors picnic after the last ornament is hung and the light strands are plugged in.

A portable table dressed in white lacy linens becomes a magical dining place in the living room. A Christmas tree illuminated with twinkling lights, a fire in the fireplace, the mantel decorated with seasonal decorations, and a carol being played on the stereo sets the scene for a memorable December dinner. Light a candle, pull up a couple of living-room chairs, open a bottle of wine, and revel in the ambience.

indoor *camping* trip

Another creative indoor picnic is one with a tent. Put up a tent in the family room near the fireplace. Bring your house plants and potted trees into the room to give it a woodsy feel, if you desire. Listen to a nature CD, and get ready for one adventurous picnic.

You can serve traditional camping food, such as hot dogs or hobo dinners. A hobo dinner is chicken or beef, carrots, potatoes, and onions—all cut into bite-sized pieces—double-wrapped in an aluminum foil pocket, then roasted over a fire until the meat is cooked and the vegetables are tender.

Or, for an element of surprise, serve a dinner that you would never expect on a "camping" trip. An appetizer of caviar, followed by steak, lobster, a baked potato, and a fine red wine, is a highly unlikely camping menu. However, its charm is found in the juxtaposition of the casual camping theme with the fancy, romantic dinner for two.

Moving
days

Moving into a house or apartment can be a very stressful event, and you are usually so busy you don't really think about what you are going to eat until mealtime rolls around and your stomach starts growling. Perhaps a new neighbor will bring a welcome lunch over, sensitive to the fact that all your pots are still in boxes and your refrigerator stands bare.

This also could be the perfect time for an indoor picnic of Chinese takeout. To prepare for your picnic without wasting precious unpacking time, simply pick a handful of flowers from the overgrown backyard, sweep a corner of the floor clean, and eat your fried rice and sweet-and-sour pork by a window. You can sit on the floor, or use the boxes for chairs and a table. It's important to relax for a few moments when taking on such a large project as moving.

*T*hose quiet, loving acts bring comfort.

Welcome a new neighbor with a homemade pizza, beverages, and disposable tableware. They will appreciate your friendliness and it will be a welcome break from unpacking.

tomato & three-cheese pizza

4 ounces ricotta cheese
½ cup asiago cheese, grated
2 tablespoons fresh basil, chopped
1 pound pizza dough
2 teaspoons basil-flavored olive oil
4 roma tomatoes, sliced
3 ounce pepperoni, sliced
2 cups mozzarella cheese

1. Mix together ricotta cheese, ¼ cup asiago cheese, and fresh basil.

2. Stretch pizza dough to fit 12" round pizza pan. Evenly spread 1 teaspoon olive oil over crust.

3. Evenly spread ricotta cheese mixture over crust. Place tomatoes, pepperoni, and mozzarella cheese on pizza. Drizzle 1 teaspoon olive oil over pizza.

4. Bake pizza 15 minutes in 425°F preheated oven. Sprinkle pizza with remaining asiago cheese and bake for additional 5–10 minutes or until cheese is melted and crust is browned.

Yield: 8 servings

chocolate fondue

12 squares (1 ounce each) semi-
    sweet baking chocolate
¾ cup heavy cream
3 tablespoons brandy or rum
9 cups fresh strawberries

1. Stir chocolate and heavy cream
in a fondue pot.

2. Stir in brandy or rum.

3. Swirl strawberries in chocolate
fondue.

Yield: 12 servings

Above: *Strawberries are being swirled in the cool chocolate above; however, other tasty treats such as cherries, peach slices, banana chunks, lady fingers, angel food and pound cake chunks also can be used.*

in bed

Your bed is the stage where many of your life's experiences happen. It is where the kids get into pillow fights, and where the cat plays underneath the sheets. It is the place where wonderful dreams are dreamt and snuggling and cuddling abounds. Your bed is a part of your most intimate moments with the one you love.

Having a picnic is another delightful experience you can have in your bed. From a traditional breakfast-in-bed with the entire family to a five-course dinner under the sheets without the kids, a picnic in bed

is a fabulous way to reconnect with those you hold dearest. For a touch of romance on a special occasion, feed your lover chocolate-covered strawberries and sip bubbly champagne.

For a more casual picnic in bed, dress the bed in comfortable flannel or cotton sheets. Invite the entire family in for supper or a popcorn party while watching a favorite sporting event on the bedroom television. For something more romantic, use satin sheets, play classical music, dim the lights and eat by candle-light. Remember the little details, such as a pretty tray, flowers, candles, music, or whatever else goes along with the theme.

for the *Children*

Picnics and children seem to go together as naturally as do Grandmother and apple pie. Whenever you think of having a group of children over to celebrate or just one child over to spend the afternoon, a picnic is a fun and easy way to serve a meal. What you must remember is that there are as many kinds of picnics, foods to be served, and places to have them as there are children. Because to children with their unlimited imaginations, anything and everything is a possibility. So with a little thought, some creativity, and a lot of enthusiasm, planning a picnic for children can be the most fun of all. Think of the children's interests, mix that with a lighthearted approach, and you will be amazed at the results of what you have created.

Plan a picnic for little girls upstairs in the "the children's room" where sunlight peeks through sheer curtains and there is a delicate yet recognizable fragrance of clean sheets mixed with crayons. The lid of the toy chest can be opened and all of the toys, dolls, and stuffed animals—both new and old, favorite and forgotten—should be invited to join.

A picnic for little boys could be outside in the backyard with its plastic pool, or in the tree house that holds all of their summer toys and hidden walkways that are their entryway to the yet unimagined. This is where they can be "superheros," or the nation's greatest fire fighters. This is the time they can eat those foods (prepared by mom) that are believed to give supernatural powers to ward off evil and provide great strength for heroic deeds.

Have a picnic for a group of children at the petting zoo where they can pack their own lunch as well as a pre-arranged "lunch" to feed the animals.

PICNIC FUN—KID STYLE

❧ Have a prepacked basket with nonperishables for those quick, pick-up-and-go picnics.

❧ Don't forget the sunscreen, insect repellent, bandages, and individually wrapped wet wipes.

❧ Bring disposable cameras and let the kids take their own photos of a terrific day. Have them developed and let them make scrapbook pages on a rainy day.

❧ Bottles of bubbles, sand buckets and shovels, jump rope, or water toys come with built-in fun.

❧ Slip in a magnifying glass, butterfly net, and a bug jar for your favorite bug collector.

❧ Purchase inexpensive Frisbees and use them for paper plate holders. When lunch is done, play Frisbee® golf.

Eating outdoors is fun for everybody, especially kids. Rules for eating outside are more lenient than eating inside. For instance, mixing play with food and speaking in an excited, loud voice are more tolerable at a picnic. You can't very well spit watermelon seeds out on the dining room carpet, yet it's expected at a picnic. While eating at the kitchen table, people typically finish their meal in one sitting. During a picnic, it may be acceptable to eat a little, and then go play for a little while before returning for more food.

caramel apples

8 small craft sticks
8 medium apples, washed and dried
4 cups sugar
2 tablespoons corn syrup
1 cup water
2 cups unsalted butter, cut into pieces, room temperature
2 cups heavy cream
Pinch of salt

1. Fill a heatproof bowl with water; this is so you can submerge bottom of saucepan in water if caramel starts to burn.

2. Insert a small craft stick into stem end of each apple. Set apples aside on waxed paper.

3. Place sugar, corn syrup, and water in heavy-bottomed, medium-sized saucepan with high sides. Stir with wooden spoon to mix. Cook over medium heat. Do not stir again until syrup becomes a deep golden amber.

4. Remove from heat. Using a clean wooden spoon, beat in butter then stir in cream. Add salt.

5. Dip apples in caramel, swirling, and tilting pan around so apples are completely coated. Return apples to waxed paper to cool and harden.

Yield: 8 servings

Picnics are not only fun, they give kids fabulous learning opportunities. They learn science through play, such as how blowing bubbles from a star-shaped wire makes spherical bubbles, not star-shaped bubbles. Or throwing a Frisbee too high means it won't travel farther. They learn other nature lessons firsthand, like the fact that ants like "people food," and they can carry food particles many times larger than their bodies.

Picnics allow kids to tap into their imaginations and learning skills while nourishing their bodies. Picnics let kids relax, as well as play hard. They enjoy nature or somewhere new while spending quality time with parents, friends, and family members. Youngsters are free to be themselves. Without a doubt, picnics and kids go together.

Picnic places for CHILDREN

Do your children have specific interests? Why not let those interests dictate the direction that your picnic will take? A picnic including toddlers will be much different than a picnic geared to the interests of nine- or ten-year-olds, or teens. Sometimes a family picnic will need to span all age groups. Here are a few ideas for clever picnics for children and youth:

❧ Local zoos and aquariums are perfect for a family picnic, since they usually have facilities for picnicking so that the day can be spent enjoying their features. Have the children dress up in clothing that has zoo animals or animal patterns on them and have a picnic menu that consists of several of the zoo animals' diets, such as cut fruit for the monkeys.

❧ A backpack lunch and an autumn hike to check out the seasonal changes is an option that most older children and teenagers will enjoy.

❧ Living-history centers are terrific places for children to visit and have hands-on experiences in the areas of farming, science, and community. Call ahead and see if the children can make a picnic for one or more of the animals, using the animals' prescribed diets.

❧ Water parks and public pools are a great way to spend a hot summer afternoon or evening, and much like the zoo, they are likely to have a picnic area. Have a costume contest using their water gear.

❧ Have a storybook-themed picnic, with food and activities based on a favorite book.

❧ Teens would love a summer solstice or nighttime star party, complete with telescope, for plotting the skies.

❧ Another teen favorite is a picnic scavenger hunt, where a picnic list is handed out and they have to scavenge the picnic items on the list before heading out to a favorite picnic site.

❧ Plan a cultural barbeque. Select ethnic foods such as carne asada burritos and tortillas with chips and salsa, fresh fruit, and horchata (Mexican rice drink) or pineapple juice to drink. Play appropriate music and fill a piñata with candy and toys for a fun activity. Have a luau with chicken tenders, Hawaiian noodles, and fresh fruit chunks (in a bowl or on bamboo skewers). The children can make candy leis while dinner is cooking.

❧ Have a nature-search picnic at a local park or waterway. A pair of binoculars and a book on the local flora and fauna will help you to identify the plants, bugs, and animals that you see on the nature search.

❧ Select your picnic site at random by spreading out a map of your town and with eyes closed, point to a destination and picnic there.

Ice cream social

For a picnic variation that children, teens, and adults alike will love, try hosting an ice cream social. Use covered picnic tables or blankets on a grassy field. Have several flavors of ice cream and toppings such as caramel, fudge, nuts, whipped cream, bananas, and maraschino cherries. The guests have the options of requesting a scoop of plain ice cream, a sundae, or a banana split. Hand each person a spoon and a napkin, and watch as everyone enjoys the refreshments.

Finish the picnic by playing water kickball. This game should be played on a grassy area in bare feet or water shoes with a soft four-square ball. Each base consists of a water task such as a sponge in a bucket of water where the runner must squeeze the wet sponge over his head before he is tagged out, or a filled kiddie swimming pool that the runner must sit in. A water slide or water-covered sheet of plastic is perfect for sliding into home. Make certain that parents know there will be water games so the children can dress accordingly.

TOPPINGS FOR ICE CREAM

Turn a simple scoop of ice cream into a colorful and extra-tasty treat. Almost any desired candy morsel can be used to top a scoop of ice cream. Here are a few topping ideas for your ice cream social:

❧ Almonds

❧ Bananas

❧ Blueberries

❧ Butterscotch sauce

❧ Caramel sauce

❧ Chocolate sauce

❧ Chocolate-covered raisins

❧ Coconut

❧ Crushed cookies

❧ Gumdrops

❧ Gummy bears

❧ Hot-fudge sauce

❧ Maraschino cherries

❧ Marshmallow sauce

❧ Peanut butter cups

❧ Peanuts

❧ Raspberries

❧ Sprinkles

❧ Strawberries

❧ Whipping cream

tea for *two*

When I was a young girl, my mother gave my sister and me a tea set. The delicate white dishes had deep blue flowers hand-painted on them, and it was put up in her china cabinet for safekeeping. I recently went home, now a mother myself, and saw the tea set sitting properly in the china cabinet, as it had for many years. It amazed me how tiny the tea set now appeared and it instantly brought back memories of my childhood.

Our mother would take the tea set from the cabinet and my sister and I would watch as she hand-washed each piece until it gleamed. Carefully, and under my mother's watchful eye, we would dry each piece with a dish towel. Then, we'd place the tea set on a wooden tray and wait patiently as Mother boiled the water on the stove. She filled the sugar dish with sugar cubes and placed homemade lemon cookies on the flat plate. When the tea was ready, we would rush over to our little art table, now covered with a white tablecloth from inside the china cabinet, and sit straight up in our chairs, cloth napkins in our laps. When our mother served the tea, we thanked her with a princess's charm and manner, and with pinky fingers pointed outward, sipped the tea. We never really liked hot tea, but we enjoyed the entire experience so much, we drank it anyway. Memories like these are etched into the mind forever.

Memories are made in moments like these.

Towering trees, green grass, and blue sky make a perfect stage for tea with great grandmother or a country picnic. Yet it simply isn't complete without the stars—the children. Bedecked in sun bonnets and costumes, summer dresses for the little ladies and shorts sets for the young men, they hospitably offer their stuffed bunnies and teddy bears sips of lemonade. This type of picnic is ideal and fairly realistic for Easter, when the children are dressed up and on their best behavior. However, getting the little tykes to participate in such a picturesque picnic will most likely be short lived. So if you are lucky enough to get your children to pose like the ones in the above photograph, make certain to snap their picture quickly. After a short while, they lose interest and run off for a game of tag, complete with grass stains and skinned knees.

children's Russian tea

2 cups imitation orange drink mix
1 3-ounce package imitation lemonade mix
1⅓ cups sugar
1 teaspoon cinnamon
½ teaspoon ground cloves

1. Combine all ingredients together and store in an airtight container.

2. Add 2–3 teaspoons of mixture to 1 cup hot water for one serving.

Yield: 25 servings

Enjoy!

A picnic means something different to everybody. Some people visualize a picnic as a romantic and personal meal shared between two lovers. Others see a picnic as a party for a group of people, where each family brings something different to eat. Everyone, however, can agree that in its simplest definition, a picnic is an occasion where everybody has fun eating food.

Sometimes, there is so much thought and preparation placed into a picnic that it loses one of its most important objectives—to be pleasurable. A picnic, especially one for children, should not be so stressful that the sight and function of the picnic is lost. If the brownies get burned moments before lunchtime, have a guest pick up a plate of brownies from the grocery store on their way. If you fret, everyone else senses your uneasiness. Furrowed brows have no place at a picnic—only smiles. So keep it simple and worry-free, and don't forget to enjoy the picnic. After all, a picnic is a good time to be had by all!

METRIC TABLES

LENGTH

metric	equivalent	imperial
1 millimetre [mm]	1 mm	0.0394 in.
1 centimetre [cm]	10 mm	0.3937 in.
1 metre [m]	100 cm	1.0936 yd.
1 kilometre[km]	1000 m	0.6214 mi.

imperial	equivalent	metric
1 inch [in.]	1 in.	2.54 cm
1 foot [ft.]	12 in.	0.3048 m
1 yard [yd.]	3 ft.	0.9144 m
1 mile [mi.]	1760 yd.	1.6093 km
1 int. nautical mi.	2025.4 yd.	1.852 km

WEIGHT

metric	equivalent	imperial
1 milligram [mg]	1 mg	0.0154 grain
1 gram [g]	1000 mg	0.0353 oz.
1 kilogram [kg]	1000 g	2.2046 lb.
1 tonne [t]	1000 kg	0.9842 ton

imperial	equivalent	metric
1 ounce [oz.]	437.5 grain	28.35 g
1 pound [lb.]	16 oz.	0.4536 kg
1 ton	20 cwt	1.016 t

VOLUME

imperial	equivalent	metric
1 teaspoon [tsp.]		5 ml
3 tsp.	1 [tbsp.]	15 ml
2 tablespoon [tbsp.]	1 fl. oz.	30 ml
1 cup	8 fl. oz.	0.24 litre [l]
2 cups	1 pint [pt.]	0.47 l
4 cups	1 quart [qt.]	0.95 l
4 qts.	1 gallon [gal.]	3.8 l
16 tbsp.	1 cup	0.24 l

imperial	UK equivalent	metric
1 fluid ounce [fl. oz.]	1.0408 UK fl. oz.	29.574 ml
1 pt.	0.8327 UK pt.	0.4731 l
1 gal.	0.8327 UK gal.	3.7854 l

TEMPERATURE CONVERSION EQUATIONS
degrees Fahrenheit (°F) to degrees Celsius (°C)

°F to °C	=	(°F - 32) x 5/9
°C to °F	=	(°C x 9/5) + 32

ACKNOWLEDGMENTS

The author would like to thank the following businesses for product donations, discounts, or photography at their business site:

Cactus & Tropicals
2735 So. 200 East
Salt Lake City, Utah 84109
801-485-2542

Cats Cradle
120 West Center St.
Provo, Utah
801-374-1832

Faye D. Foster
Antiques & Interiors
4 Central Square, Unit 2
Bristol, New Hampshire 03222
603-744-9130

La Niche Gourmet & Gifts
401 So. Main Street
Park City, Utah 84060
435-649-2372

Pfaff Sewing Machines
610 Winters Ave.
Paramus, New Jersey 07653
www.pfaff-us-cda.com

Poison Creek
Antique & Art Gallery
95 So. Main Street
Kamas, Utah
435-783-6655

State of Utah
Department of Parks and Recreation
Wasatch Mountain State Park

Sugar House Antiques
2120 S. Highland Dr.
Salt Lake City, Utah 84106
801-487-5084

Sunset Ranch Stables
Indoor Arena
Banquet Room
Pinedale, Wyoming
307-367-6221

Traces
Garden Supplies
1432 So. 1100 E.
Salt Lake City, Utah 84105

The publisher wishes to thank the following for use of their projects, homes, businesses, or photographs:

Corbis Corporation Images: (© 1998, 1999, 2000, 2001)

Dietrich Stock Photo: p 119
Wickenburg, Arizona 85358
e-mail: dietrich@w3az.net

Jill Grover: pp 34, 36, 37

Michael Lutch: pp 70–71
Milton, Massachusetts
e-mail: michael@lutchphoto.com

Carol and Chip Nelson: p 113

Leslie Newman: pp 14, 15, 30–31, 92–93
Scotland, Connecticut
e-mail: LNewman900@aol.com

Robert Perron: p 82

Photodisc, Inc. Images (© 1992, 1993, 1994, 1995, 1996, 1998, 1999, 2000, 2001)

INDEX

Accessories, and the **24–43**
Acknowledgments 131
Along the Water's Edge 54–55
Antique Road Trip 102–103
Autumn Fare 76–77

backyard . . . 28, 45, 55, 59, 64, 73, 96,
    114, 118
Backyard Picnic 73–75
Biker Lunch 107
breakfast 48, 78, 83, 94–96

children . . .8, 12, 37, 45, 58–59, 67, 86,
    118, 121–124, 129
china . . . 20, 27–28, 53, 65, 84, 86, 126
China or Not 27–29
Christmas Picnic, a 110–111
Chuckwagon Breakfast Ideas 95
condiments 30, 107
Country Garden Picnic 72
Custom Tablecloth 40

Enjoy .129
European Pleasures 84–85

Fitted Table Topper 39
Folded Napkin Silverware Pocket . . 41
For a Crowd 58–59
For a Picnic **44–59**
For the Children **118–129**

Ice Cream Social 124–125
In a Tepee 92–93
In Bed 116–117
In the Basket **10–23**
In the Garden **60–77**
In the Greenhouse 88–89
In the Home **108–117**
In the Snow 98–99
In the Woods **52–59**
In Unusual Places **86–99**
Include Local Specialties 48–49
indoor 109–110, 112, 114

Indoor Camping Trip 112–113
Introduction 8–9

Linens Linens Linens 39–43
Metric Tables 130
More Than One Use 34–37
morning 60, 83, 94, 96
Morning Air 82–83
Moving Days 114–115

Not Your Regular Sack Lunch 17

Ocean Side 104–105
Old-fashioned Charm 68–69
On the Porch **78–85**
On the Range 94–97
On the Road **100–107**
On-the-Road Tips 107
On the Rooftop 90–91
On the Trail 56–57

park 45, 59, 86, 106–107
Pass the Condiments 30–31
Perfect Picnic Basket, the 20–21
Picnic Destinations 116–117
Picnic Fun—Kid Style 120
Picnic Places for Children . . . 122–123
Picnic Safety Tips 22–23
Picnic Serving Dishes 32–33
Plate Holder Pocket 42
porch 65, 67, 83, 85, 109
potluck 45, 59
Potlucking It 59

Recipes:
    caramel apples 121
    children's Russian tea 128
    chocolate fondue 116
    flavored butters 75
       herb garden & spice butter . . 75
       Santa Fe chipotle butter 75
    fresh lemonade 65

frosted lemon shortbread cookies
   65
    gazpacho 105
    grilled corn in the husks 75
    hearty pumpkin soup 76
    homemade ice cream 68
    on-the-trail Coney dogs 57
    orange stick fondue 32
    provencal pasta 85
    range lasagna 97
    simmering chicken soup 99
    tomato & three-cheese pizza . .115
    Uncle Jack's Dutch oven corn bread
   103
rooftop 91

Selecting a Site 46–47
spring 45, 70, 76, 80
Springtime Buffet 80–81
summer 46, 53, 76, 100, 118,
    122–123, 128
Swing Picnic 66–67

tablecloth 8, 11, 20, 24, 36, 39–40,
    44, 53, 56, 59, 68, 71– 72, 78, 86,
    100,106, 126
Tailgate Picnic, a 106
Take a Detour 50–51
Tea for Two 126–128
tepee 93
theme 70–71, 76, 85–86, 91, 112,
    117, 123
Theme Picnic 70–71
Things to Consider 22–23
Toppings for Ice Cream 125
Types of Baskets 12–23

Wine Bottle & Glass Holder
    Pocket 43
winter 53, 98–99